PM Traditi
Tales and I
TEACHERS' GUIDE

Silver Level

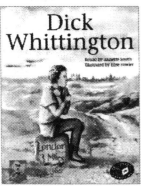

STEPHANIE DIX

NELSON PRICE MILBURN

Contents

About the PM Library

Story Books, Traditional Tales and Plays, and Animal Facts

The basic philosophy

'Children learn best with books that have meaning and are rewarding' … *Reading in Junior Classes*, New Zealand Department of Education.

'I can read this!' All books in the PM Library are **centred on meaning**, but they are also designed to give children the rewarding experience of **success**. If a child can read one book they should be able to read another and another. Success should follow success. When the right match of 'child to book' is made, the greater the child's interest and the greater his or her desire to read.

On every page in every book care is taken with the sentence structures, the choice of words, the clear well-spaced type, and with the meaningful, accurate illustrations. Because the books are easy as well as interesting, children are able to practise a variety of reading skills and enjoy the feedback of success. They learn new words — and practise them again and again — all the time understanding what they are reading about, and returning to the books with pleasure *because* they have real meaning, and emotional impact.

The criticism levelled at many 'stories' written for beginners is that most are not stories — they are highly repetitious reading exercises in which meaning comes a poor second. Teachers and children have often been disappointed by the bland banality of most early school 'readers', with pages that were shaped not by a storyteller but by a need to repeat known words, or sentence structures or letter clusters, as often as possible. In revulsion from these interest-starved, over-repetitive non-literary exercises, some modern teachers have built their reading programs around library picture books that are worth reading for their own sake — only to discover that too many children are defeated when presented with 200 or so basic words in quick succession. It is not easy for average beginners to sort out *were was with will well would who why what when where which went want won't walk watch wall wait work wash warm word* … it never will be!

The authors of the PM Library have worked hard to combine the virtues of two approaches — **controlled basic vocabulary** to let children master a growing number of common but confusing **high frequency** words, and **storytelling** quality to engage the mind and emotions and make learning to read satisfying. The authors have been well supported by a team of highly talented illustrators.

Features of the PM Story Books

The books have many ingredients, and all stories are rigorously considered and shaped to meet high standards.

All stories have:
- *meaningful content*. The situations and concepts can be understood by young children. The resolution in each story is logical — these stories encourage children to think by *letting* them think. The books are full of opportunities for intelligent discussion and logical prediction.
- *well-shaped plots*. Tension appears early in each story — something goes amiss — and the problem is solved by the end. It is tension that keeps children and teachers interested in the story — what will happen next? When the problem is finally resolved the ending is satisfying.
- *no sexism, racism or stereotyping of people*. Some women have supportive roles but others work — there is a female police officer and a female engineer. Jack's dad is a caregiver. Black, Asian and Caucasian children all have a turn at being central characters. The books include a boy with Down's syndrome, and a girl and a boy who use a wheelchair, and the elderly, too, are shown leading active lives.
- *a wide spread of subjects* to meet the different experiences and enthusiasms of as many children as possible. There are stories about everyday life at home in the suburbs and at school; some stories are set in the inner city and others in the great outdoors. Toby, the tow truck who advises his driver, introduces readers to technology; this is fantasy that lifts children's understanding of the modern world.
  Another subset takes children back to the days of the dinosaurs; other stories look at modern animals (from elephants and beavers to guinea pigs and goldfish). Common natural crises — hailstorms, thunder, lightning and the pitch black night — provide drama and should help children face their fears, just as the characters in the stories do.
- *warmth and emotional sensitivity*. The child heroes are successful problem solvers — they are never laughed at, and never made to look inadequate. Animals are treated with sensitivity, too.
- *language that is satisfying to the ear*. The rhythms of good English — storyteller's English — are there. These stories pass the test of good literature and they sound satisfying when they are read aloud. The power of these stories is enhanced by balanced phrasing, and the right word in the right place.

- **considerable scientific accuracy**. Because accuracy matters, the dinosaur stories are carefully written to reflect recent research, and Toby the tow truck solves his towing problems in technically accurate ways. **All** stories are checked for accuracy.
- **well-designed typography**. At this level a serifed type face gives words coherence and individuality. The spacing of words, lines and paragraphs enhances readability. The classic typeface has been selected for its exceptional readability.
- **elisions**. These continue to be consolidated.
- **a rate of new word introduction strictly held to 1 in 20**. When each new word is supported by at least 19 known words the decoding process is easier. Children are reading well away from frustration level. They are at a success level where reading is enjoyed. They are reading for pleasure and meaning. By Silver Level, children will have mastered more than 600 high frequency (heavy duty) words as well as many *interest* words. It is reassuring to know that these high frequency words account for about 80% of the words used in most passages of narrative English written for adults.
- **many opportunities to learn about the way words work**. At this stage of their reading children have to be able to turn written letters into spoken sounds, continue the sounds and check the message. The reading process depends on all three skills. When faced by a new word children need to be shown how to break it into syllables or letter clusters. Successful decoders have to be flexible and have enough confidence to keep trying. Confidence is built from past successes, from application of syntactic and semantic cues, and from mastery of words and letter clusters met before. Through experience, children will become aware that the vowel **a** is likely to represent one of five sounds: *a* as in *at*, or *ah*, or *ape* or *all*, or *ago*. In English it is flexibility that leads to successful decoding.
- **attractive well-drawn illustrations** that enable children to gain maximum understanding as they match picture with text, and vice versa. Meticulous care has been taken with these hardworking pictures. These are books that children will return to again and again with delight.

Features of the PM Traditional Tales and Plays

- **Although these stories are simplified short versions of the well-known tales, a great deal of the original flavour has been kept.** Most of the tales have been firmly anchored in time and place so that *Dick Whittington* is clearly English, *Androcles and the Lion* reflects the harshness and injustices of the time in which it was written, and *The Elves and the Shoemaker* and *Puss-in-Boots* both belong to the 17th century.

- **Each part in each play** is colour coded to lessen confusion and help children understand the conventions of a printed play.

Features of PM Animal Facts

- **Vocabulary is linked to the grading of the Story Books and Traditional Tales and Plays**. The grading logo, a coloured petal, indicates the recommended level for Guided Reading. As with the Story Books and Traditional Tales and Plays, the introduction of each new word is supported by 19 known words.
- **Non-fiction has a different 'dialect'**. Many sentences are short, and the necessary introduction of new interest words (mostly nouns) is accompanied by exact picture clues. Children reading non-fiction have to learn to link photographs and text and 'read' them together, as both inform. Each paragraph stands alone. Children do not have to hold the thread of a story in their minds as they read — pages can sometimes be read out of order, and the book approached through its index. All these things (short sentences, abundance of picture clues, absence of a developing plot) mean that many children find non-fiction less demanding than fiction, and even more enjoyable.
- **Non-fiction has a standard layout**, with new components that can be explored in PM Animal Facts, e.g. contents page, clear headings, labelled diagrams, alphabetical index.
- **A linear self-correcting program.** The questions at the foot of the page are not designed to make children research other books, nor to 'trick' them. Their purpose is to build confidence and to secure information. The immediate re-reading of a page of text to find or check an answer leads to careful thought, and greater retention of knowledge.
- **PM non-fiction books have reliable information**. Thorough research and scientific accuracy matter in all books in the PM Library, not least in the non-fiction books.
- **High interest levels**. In spite of their simplicity, these books arouse interest, e.g. Did you know that … male emperor penguins look after their offspring for the first nine weeks? … a blue whale weighs the same as 25 elephants? … male caribou shed their antlers in winter? Even adults will learn something new.
- **Independent research**. The simplicity of the text and the clarity of the layout allows young children to taste the delights of independent discovery.
- **Links with the PM Story Books** increase children's understanding, adding depth to both strands. Many PM Story Books are supported by non-fiction titles: *Nelson Gets a Fright* is matched with *Elephants* (PM Animal Facts: Animals in the Wild); *Silver and Prince* is matched with *Wolves* (PM Animal Facts: Polar Animals).

Using this Teachers' Guide

Before beginning the PM Story Books at Silver Level, children will have read the PM Story Books at the Orange, Turquoise, Purple and Gold levels. They will have acquired more than 600 high frequency words and a very wide range of interest words. These books will have allowed the children to develop confidence, skills and independence, and to think critically about language and meaning. Predictability and logic are an essential part of these stories. It is this strong focus on logic and sense that helps children form the habit of self-correction. **Meaning** is the most important element in all PM Story Books.

The Teachers' Guides have been designed to assist busy teachers to plan and develop challenging language opportunities in their classrooms. The PM Story Books should be used with a wide variety of other books and materials to ensure that children succeed at each level before they proceed to the next. The ideas described in each Teachers' Guide can be adapted for other books.

There are Teachers' Guides for each colour level.

The eight oval shapes show the more advanced levels that follow the large daisy logo. The levels are: Silver Level 23, Silver Level 24; Emerald Level 25, Emerald Level 26; Ruby Level 27, Ruby Level 28; Sapphire Level 29, Sapphire Level 30.

Level

23
24
25
26
27
28
29
30

By the end of Silver Level, children should have reading ages of 8½–9 years.

Each Teachers' Guide has suggestions and ideas for guidance in the use of the PM books at that level. Emphasis has been placed upon the development of the language skills — speaking, listening, reading, writing, viewing and presenting. These skills are common to all curriculum areas. Reading is not treated as a subject that stands alone.

Creating the atmosphere

This is the 'tuning in' stage. It is the time when the teacher focuses the children's thinking on the content or concepts of the tale. At this stage, related language or exciting new vocabulary can be discussed, written on the whiteboard or sometimes acted out. In this way new ideas become familiar and the children's language is enriched.

Focusing on the tale

Guided reading

Book study is an in-depth study of the tale. It is a time to follow the plot, to become emotionally involved in the tension, the climax and above all to enjoy — perhaps predict — the satisfying ending.

It should be such an enjoyable experience that the children will want to read the tale right through to the end all by themselves. Because new high frequency words have been introduced slowly and carefully in the tales children can achieve this success.

Going beyond the tale

Teachers may select from or adapt these language enrichment activities to suit the needs of their own classes. Some activities are suitable for small groups of children to work at together, others are for individuals. Some may even be taken with a whole class. All have been designed to develop purposeful stimulating language. They give children ample opportunity to interact verbally not only with teachers but also with one another. The art and drama activities will allow children opportunities to express themselves and help them to make sense of their reading.

Books to share and compare

These are suggested titles of books by other authors and from other publishers. Children need to have many stories read to them, often. They soon know that reading is enjoyable and will want to return to favourite books to read themselves. Occasional questions about the stories will sharpen the focus, prompt interest and talk, and ensure that children listen with understanding.

Reading aloud to children is one of the best ways of enriching their vocabulary and increasing their general knowledge.

Blackline masters

Blackline masters of mask templates for most characters in the plays have been included in this Teachers' Guide. Making masks will provide children with opportunities for:

- reading and following instructions
- co-operative problem solving

- mathematical discussion about proportion
- individual creativity.

It is recommended that the templates be photocopied onto lightweight card. A headband to secure the mask can be made from a 3 cm strip of card long enough to fit around the child's head. Secure the strip of card to each side of the mask.

Plays

The plays can be read by children with the reading and analytical skills required at Silver Level; the structures and words used are those that they can read with confidence. Each play should also be able to be read with understanding because the tale which the play is based on has just been read in guided reading (it is easier for children to act out a familiar story). In addition, the plays can also be read by young children who are looking at a play script for the first time. The coloured panels, which indicate particular characters, let the children know when their parts appear.

The tales and plays at
Silver Level

Level

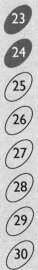

23
24
25
26
27
28
29
30

The Strange Shoe

As in all fables there is a moral:
'It is difficult to take in ideas, however valid, that are well beyond our experience.'

Children who read this tale should be able to appreciate the animals' puzzlement, and look at themselves in a new way.

The fable has been retold from *Short Stories About Animals*, London, 1882.

Setting: an Indian jungle

Era: mythical past

Creating the atmosphere

- Read and discuss *The Hare and the Tortoise* (PM Traditional Tales and Plays Purple Level). In particular, focus on the disagreement between the hare and the tortoise. Encourage the children to talk about any disagreements or differences of opinions that they may have had with a friend or friends. What did they argue about and how did they find a solution?

Focusing on the tale — guided reading

- Study the cover illustration and read the title together. Discuss the characters depicted, and talk about the link between the illustration and the title. Encourage reasoning.
- pp.2–3 — Use visual clues and discuss the setting; then use an atlas to locate India — the setting of the story. Ensure that the children understand the meaning of the term *mystery*.
- pp.4–7 — Talk about both characters as they are introduced. Have the children read these pages silently in order to find out what the bear and the tiger think the strange object is. Compare their different ideas and their reasoning.
- pp.8–11 — Encourage the children to predict what the monkey and the deer think the mystery object is. Have them read silently and then talk about their predictions. Discuss the meanings of the words *inquisitive, scampered, snatched.*
- pp.12–13 — Have the children read p.12 silently to find out if the wolf agreed with any of the other animals. Ask the children to explain the argument in the story. Can they think of a way the animals could come to an agreement? Have the children locate and read the words (verbs) that show how the animals argued with each other, e.g. *shouted, growled,* etc.
- pp.14–17 — Examine the illustrations and discuss the animals' facial expressions. Talk about how the owl describes 'man'. Is it a good description? (Discuss the term *man* as a general word meaning 'humankind'.) Have the children recall the reasons why the animals don't believe owl. Ensure that they understand the terms *ridiculous, absurd, scoffed.*
- pp.18–20 — Encourage the children to read these pages silently in order to find out how the story ends. Describe the techniques that the author used to show that the animals were angry. Talk about owl's feelings when no one believed her.

Going beyond the tale

- As a class, re-read the tale. In pairs, have the children locate the words that describe each animal. Record these, and then share and compare.
- Discuss the term 'argument' (as in a discussion in which reasons are put forward) in its oral and written form. Ask the children to give real-life examples where they might hear or read an 'argument'. Give the class one of the following statements and divide them into two groups. Ask them to write an argument either supporting or negating the statement. Encourage them to support their opinions with logical and sound reasoning. Alternatively, organise a class debate on one of the following statements.
  — School uniforms should be compulsory.
  — Children should learn a musical instrument at school.
  — The school café should sell only healthy food.

- Discuss how the tale could be continued. What might happen when the animals see people — people who are wearing shoes? Ask the children to continue the narrative in written form and then share 'part two' during a group conference. Ensure that the children know how to set out and record direct speech.
- There are many strange and interesting forms of footwear that are or have been worn by different groups of people. In pairs, have the children brainstorm and record what they know. Encourage them to then use a range of information sources to research the topic further. Ensure that the children have the skills required to use library catalogues, the Internet and book indexes. Encourage them to contact shoe shops or other experts to locate pictures and relevant information. Have the children present their information in a visually interesting way.

> Show children how to search and extract information from a variety of sources.

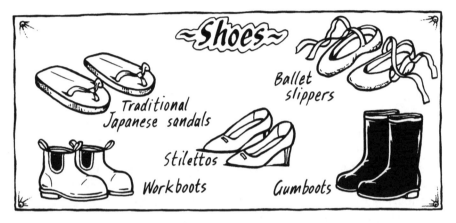

- Using a variety of scrap materials, have the children construct a mural of an Indian jungle. Encourage them to use the library or the Internet to research the types of plants that grow there and other animals that live in an Indian jungle.
- Discuss the fact that the owl is not believed even though she is telling the truth. Talk about how she would feel and what she could do to make the other animals believe her. Point out that we all have different opinions or points of view based on personal knowledge and experiences. Encourage the children to listen to each other's points of view and value all contributions during classroom discussions.
- Revisit the tale. Turn to p.21 and direct the children to use the play format. In groups of seven, have each child take on a character role. Encourage them to practise their part using appropriate intonation and expression. Have the children produce the play using a variety of technologies, e.g. by using stick puppets, or by using an overhead projector, screen and shadow puppets to retell the story.

> Reinforce that visual information is another important form of language communication.

Books to share and compare

- *Kuia and the Spider,*
  Patricia Grace,
  Puffin, 1982.
- *Seven Blind Mice,*
  Ed Young,
  Philomel Books, 1992.
- *The Hare and the Tortoise,*
  retold by Jenny Giles,
  PM Traditional Tales and Plays
  Purple Level,
  Nelson ITP, 1998.
- *The King of the Birds,*
  Helen Ward,
  Koala Books, 1997.

Aesop, a Greek slave who lived about 550 BC, told a version of this fable. The story was later resited in ancient Rome, where runaway slaves and criminals were often forced to fight wild animals in the arena.

The fable has a satisfying moral: 'A kindness is often repaid.' This, as well as its strong drama, has made it a popular story for many centuries.

Setting: North Africa and Rome

Era: about 140 BC

Androcles and the Lion

Creating the atmosphere

- Collect and display factual books depicting life in ancient Roman times. Encourage the children to compare and discuss their own lifestyles with those of ancient Rome, examining such differences as home life, dress, buildings and occupations. Talk about the way the ancient Roman class system was organised and how slaves had to carry out tasks for their wealthy owners.

Focusing on the tale — guided reading

- Ask the children to briefly look through the book and predict the story line. Encourage them to predict what the relationship might be between the lion and Androcles.
- pp.2–3 — Have the children read these pages silently. Ask them to:
  — record the characteristics that describe Androcles (the main character)
  — consider how they would feel if they were a slave
  — explain their understanding of the word *trust*.
- pp.4–7 — Ask the children to read these pages silently and then:
  — provide the reasons why Androcles ran away
  — discuss his escape plan
  — share any words they do not understand, e.g. *fled, barren, exhausted*.
- pp.8–11 — Have the children read these pages silently. As a group, discuss how the children would have felt if they were Androcles and had been woken by a roaring lion. Direct them to locate and read the words in the text describing how Androcles felt. Discuss the friendship between the lion and Androcles, and the trust that developed between them.
- pp.12–17 — Examine the illustration on p.17. Ask the children to predict what may happen to Androcles. Have them then read pp.12–17 silently. Ask the children to:
  — discuss the Roman soldiers and the job they had to do
  — identify Androcles's crime and punishment; compare both these with some of our less serious crimes of today and how society deals with them.
- pp.18–20 — Have the children read these pages silently. Ask them to:
  — share with a partner how the story ended
  — explain the reactions of the noisy crowd
  — discuss the meaning of the text, 'Androcles could live without fear.'

Going beyond the tale

- Provide other stories which explore the friendships that can develop between people and animals, e.g. *Grey Friars Bobby, Black Beauty, Dick Whittington* (PM Traditional Tales and Plays Silver Level). Encourage the children to read these books independently. Have them keep a record of the books they read in a reading log. They can then meet in a 'reading circle' to report on their books and to 'sell' them to other readers.

- Revisit the tale, specifically to study the illustrations of the soldiers (in particular, focus on their uniforms and weaponry). Encourage the children to find out more about the life of a Roman soldier during this period of history. Have them write questions that will form the basis of their research. Display the children's findings on the wall along with their research questions and relevant illustrations.

Demonstrate the skills of gathering, organising and presenting information.

What was the role of a Roman soldier?

What was their armour made from?

What kind of weapons did they use?

- Display a world map in the classroom. Have the children use reference books on ancient Rome to find out about the Roman Empire and identify those countries which would be in the Roman Empire if it still existed today.
- As entertainment the ancient Romans enjoyed visual spectacles where men physically competed against animals. Discuss the festivals or events where this still happens today, e.g. bullfights, rodeo riding, lion and elephant hunting. Model how to develop and write an argument for or against, for example, bullfighting. On strips of paper, have the children write statements with supporting arguments for or against this type of activity. They can then paste their statements under the relevant heading. Discuss and value each person's opinion.

Contribute to discussions respecting the views of others.

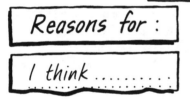

Bullfighting

Reasons for :

I think . . . .

Reasons against :

I think . . . .

- Identify the key ideas in the story and show the children how to record them as a 'mind map'. Encourage them to use these key ideas to confidently retell the story in their own words developing and embellishing each part. Invite the children to visit a junior class and become oral 'storytellers' retelling the traditional tale, *Androcles and the Lion*, in their own unique way.
- People keep unusual pets. Have the children locate some 'unusual pet' stories or appropriate pictures in magazines and newspapers. Display the information in the classroom and encourage the children to read or retell the stories. These articles could then be used as 'starters' for writing narratives about unusual pets and their adventures.
- Androcles had to face many fears. On a chart, record what they were and their outcomes. Ask the children to share and then write about their own fears.
- Revisit the tale. Turn to p.21 and direct the children to use the play format. Organise the class into groups and encourage each member to take a character role and practise their part using appropriate intonation and expression. Groups can produce the play using a variety of technologies, e.g by using a tape recorder to make a radio play (encourage the use of sound effects).

Books to share and compare

- *The Story of Ferdinand,*
  Munro Leaf,
  Puffin, 1967.
- *The Biggest Bear,*
  Lyn Ward,
  Houghton Mifflin, 1988.
- *The Lion and the Mouse,*
  Gerald Rose,
  Cambridge University Press, 1996.
- *Grey Friars Bobby,*
  Ruth Brown,
  Andersen Press, 1995.
- *Black Beauty,*
  Anna Sewell,
  Golden Pleasure Books, 1963.

The Bear and the Trolls

This story is a retelling of *The Cat on the Dovrefell* (from *Popular Tales from the Norse* by Asbjörsen and Moe, translated 1859). The trolls of Norwegian folklore were highly mischievous and this traditional tale captures their character.

Setting: Norway

Era: about 1800

Creating the atmosphere

- Read the traditional tale *The Three Billy Goats Gruff* (PM Traditional Tales and Plays Orange Level). Have the children act out the story by role-playing the three goats and the nasty troll who lived under the bridge.

Focusing on the tale — guided reading

- Study the cover illustration and read the title. Have the children use the illustration to describe the trolls. Anticipate the kind of characters they might be.
- pp.2–3 — Discuss the forest setting. How is it similar/different to our native bush? Talk about the man's clothes and in which country the story may be set. Have the children read these pages independently to identify the main characters and establish the story's setting.
- p.4–7 — Ask the children to 'skim' read the text on p.4 to locate the woodcutter's name. Have them read pp.4–7 silently to identify both Finn's and Halvor's problem. Discuss how each problem could be solved. Ask the children to describe the trolls, supporting their descriptions with words from the text. Ensure that they understand the intensity of winter time in the far north and that they know what is meant by the 'shortest day of the year'. Discuss how the illustrator has created the effect of coldness.
- pp.8–9 — Read and discuss Finn's solution to his problem. Consider what he might do if the trolls come in.
- pp.10–13 — Examine the illustrations. Have the children describe the trolls and their mischievous deeds. Read the text to find out when and how they got inside the cottage, and the types of food they consumed. Ensure that the children understand the phrases and terms *stroke of midnight, shutters, jostling, salt herrings, rafters*.
- pp.14–17 — Predict how Björn felt about being woken up. Have the children read these pages silently. Locate the words that tell how Björn reacted to being teased, and the words describing the actions of the terrified trolls. Discuss why it was such an amusing tale for Finn to tell Halvor and his family.
- pp.18–20 — Ask the children to read these pages independently and then retell the story's ending to a partner.

Going beyond the tale

- Invite the children to continue the tale by describing what the mischievous trolls got up to next. Have them work independently or with a partner to produce 'part two' of the tale as a storyboard or picture strip. Encourage them to begin their tale with 'It was Midwinter's Eve...'.
- Revisit the tale to find words describing the trolls' physical appearances, behaviours and personalities. Write these words on a chart and invite the children to add more to the 'word bank'. Encourage each child to use crayons to draw their own troll character. Have them cut it out and paste it onto a class mural. The children can then paste a character description of their troll next to their drawing.
- Re-read p.12. As a group, list the food the trolls ate. Ask the children to brainstorm the types of food they would like to feast upon in the middle of a cold winter's night. On a new list, write down their responses. Compare the two lists.

> Record and present information in a different form.

- Invite a group of children to create 'snow music' using various musical instruments (bought and made). Recreate Midwinter Night with Björn and Finn curled up fast asleep. Have other children mime the trolls' actions on the stroke of midnight. Change the music accordingly.

Communicate ideas using drama.

- Find and display other tales written and set in Scandinavian countries. If possible, locate audio books of such tales, or have the children read and make their own tape recordings (using sound effects and background music). Encourage the class to listen to and enjoy a range of traditional tales.
- Poor Halvor and his family had to suffer the trolls' mischief every year. Discuss their mischievous actions from Halvor's point of view. Ask the children to take his point of view and write a letter to the trolls explaining how their behaviour is upsetting him and his family. The children can publish their letters and 'nail' them to a tree cut-out displayed in the classroom.

Provide opportunities for children to write in different text forms.

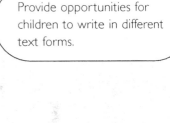

- Have the children use the library's catalogue system to locate books on white, black and brown bears. Read and compare information on the different bears. Have the children suggest appropriate headings to use for these comparisons.
- Revisit the tale using the play format on p.21. Encourage each child to take on a character role and practise their part using appropriate intonation, pitch, pace and volume. Have the children produce the play using a variety of technologies, e.g. the play could be acted out with the performers organising costumes and videoing their performance. The video could be viewed by other classes.

Books to share and compare

- *The Tomten*,
  Astrid Lindgren,
  Constable Young, 1967.
- *The Fox and the Tomten*,
  Astrid Lindgren,
  Kestrel Books, 1966.
- *Engrin and the Hungry Troll*,
  Amanda Walsh,
  Lothian, 1988.
- *The Trolls New Jersey*,
  Lyn McConchie,
  Stone Press, 1997.

The Robin Hood legend is part fact and part fiction. A yeoman turned outlaw, Robin Hood, lived in Barnsdale Forest (adjoining Sherwood) early in the 14th century. His exploits were described in popular ballads, of which a few have survived.

Confusion was caused by later writers. By 1600, the Robin Hood of the ballads had been fused, in new stories, with an earlier outlaw of noble birth.

Setting: Nottingham (England)

Era: about 1320

Robin Hood and the Silver Trophy

Creating the atmosphere

- Examine the trophies that your school presents to students each year. Discuss what the trophies represent and what the students need to achieve in order to 'win' them. Talk about the hard work and practice required to become a skilled expert in a particular field or event.

Focusing on the tale — guided reading

- Explain to the children that this tale is most probably based on true stories of a yeoman turned outlaw, Robin Hood, who lived in Barnsdale Forest (adjoining Sherwood) early in the 14th century. Have the children predict what the tale will be about by examining the cover illustration and reading the title. Examine the illustrations in the book briefly to establish the story setting.
- pp.2–3 — Have the children read p.2 silently. Talk about the Sheriff of Nottingham and the type of person he was. Ensure that the children have an understanding of the social structures of the time, and the poverty and restrictions placed on the peasants.
- pp.4–5 — Look at the illustration on p.5 and ask the children to predict reasons why the outlaws wore green and brown costumes, and used bows and arrows. Invite the children to read p.4 independently to confirm or re-evaluate their ideas. Discuss the sport of archery. Have the children share any knowledge they may have on this sport. Invite them to imagine that they are the sheriff and have them devise a plan to capture the outlaws.
- pp.6–7 — Have the children read p.6 independently to find out the sheriff's plan. Discuss the idea and meaning of Robin being 'unable to resist'.
- pp.8–9 — Ask the children to read these pages in order to find out the names of the other outlaws and to establish if the sheriff's plan is working so far. Talk about how Robin's friends respond to the news of the contest. Discuss the meanings of the words *contest, persuade, advice, fair competition, disguise*.
- pp.10–13 — Explore the visual information on these pages. Ask the children to:
  — discuss the detail of the costumes and the organisation of the contest
  — predict how Robin Hood will infiltrate the contest
  — read independently and then discuss their predictions
  — talk about the excitement that the two finalists must have felt.
- pp.14–17 — Have the children read these pages silently to find out what happens. In pairs, have each child describe to their partner the events and the outcome of the competition.
- pp.18–20 — Discuss how the crowd of people might help Robin to escape. Ask the children to read these pages silently in order to find out how they actually did help. Explain the meanings of the words *striding, capture, surging, milling, thickets, clearing, outwitted*. Discuss why Robin Hood and his fellow outlaws were so popular amongst the peasants. Explain the significance of the silver trophy.

Going beyond the tale

Reinforce learning in a variety of ways.

- Gather other stories about Robin Hood. Find books, poetic ballads and videos about the famous outlaw. Through reading and viewing, encourage the children to build up and write a detailed character sketch of Robin Hood.

- Encourage the children to research the sport of archery. They will need to write key questions that form the basis of their research, and plan where and how they will go about getting this information. Demonstrate how to note take from reading, viewing or interviewing sources.

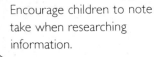Encourage children to note take when researching information.

- Have the children choose a scene from the story and recreate it as diorama. They will need a shoebox, paints or crayons and card in order to make three-dimensional stand-up figures and scenery.

- Create a 'Wanted' poster. Have the children discuss Robin Hood's characteristics — both the positive and the negative. Invite them to take a point of view and plan and construct a 'Wanted' poster of Robin Hood from the sheriff's perspective, the peasants' perspective or from the outlaws' point of view. Each poster will need to present a strong case either for or against Robin Hood.

Encourage children to view situations from a range of different perspectives.

- In small groups, invite the children to design a target game. They will need to establish the purpose of the game, the equipment needed and the rules involved. Have them discuss the design of the target, and appropriate and safe objects for throwing, e.g. paper darts, beanbags or soft balls. Encourage the children to present the instructions on how to play the game in written form, after testing and refining the procedures and rules involved.

Discuss and plan projects co-operatively and refine procedures.

- Discuss the children's camping experiences — in particular, cooking on an open fire. Allow them to share their guiding or scouting experiences and to explain orally (or in written form) how to make a fire in the ground and to cook safely outdoors.
- Robin Hood competed for and won the silver trophy. Ask the children to talk about any competitions that they have entered. Emphasise the importance of trying your best and that winning is not always the most important factor. Have the children write an imaginary or real story about a competitive event where they did/did not win a trophy. Encourage them to describe their feelings and the excitement of the event.
- Revisit the tale using the play format on p.21. Encourage each child to take on a character role and practise their part using appropriate intonation and expression. Have the children produce the play using a variety of technologies, e.g. they could act out the play using added background sound effects. The class could collect appropriate music or record sounds, e.g. birds in the forest, a variety of crowd noises, a trumpet playing.

Books to share and compare

- *The Birthday Burglar,* Margaret Mahy, Dent, 1984.
- *Hey Robin,* Robert Leeson, Black, 1989.
- *Burglar Bill,* Janet & Allan Ahlberg, Fontana, 1979.
- *Cops and Robbers,* Janet & Allan Ahlberg, Mammoth, 1989.
- *A Barrel of Gold,* Joy Cowley, Shortland Publications, 1984.
- *Georgie and the Robbers,* Robert Bright, Scholastic, 1963.

The Sleeping Beauty

Charles Perrault was an early collector of fairy tales. His version of *The Sleeping Beauty*, published in 1697, had a complex and chilling ending, involving ogres. The simpler modern version of the tale has proved to be one of the most romantic of the traditional fairy tales.

Setting: small European Kingdom

Era: 15th century

Creating the atmosphere

- Ask the children if they know anyone who has lived for one hundred years. Have them calculate how many years it will be before they turn one hundred years old. Discuss periods of time, and in particular, the relationship between years, decades and a century.

Focusing on the tale — guided reading

- Have the children retell the story of Sleeping Beauty as they remember it. They can tape their version and compare it with this tale once it has been read. Discuss the cover illustration and read the title.
- pp.2–3 — Read the text and discuss the illustration. Talk about the characters, the story's setting and the period of time. Encourage the children to support their ideas with examples from both the text and the illustration.
- pp.4–7 — Ask the children to read these pages silently. Talk about the reasons for having a naming ceremony. Ask the children to:
  — discuss any unfamiliar words
  — talk about godmothers, who they are and what they do
  — explain why the wicked fairy felt jealous and how the youngest fairy was able to save the princess from dying
  — anticipate the actions of the king.
- pp.8–11 — Direct the children to read these pages silently and retell the story (so far) to a partner. Talk about the physical features of the castle, e.g. the long passages, winding stairs and the turret. Have the children predict what will happen next.
- pp.12–15 — Ask the children to read these pages independently to confirm their predictions. Discuss the meanings of the words *disguise, ladies-in-waiting, curse, slumber*. Examine the illustration on pp.14–15. Talk about what everyone might have been doing before the fairy put them all to sleep.
- pp.16–20 — Have the children read these pages silently. Talk about the 'predicability' and 'magic' of such fairy tales, and why we like these types of stories to end 'happily ever after'.

Going beyond the tale

- Find out what the children know about spinning and how the spinning wheel works to make thread. Invite an expert into the classroom to demonstrate.
- As a class, brainstorm and list information about castles. Encourage the children to research the topic further by visiting the library to locate reference books and materials. Ensure that the children know how to locate relevant information. In small groups, invite the children to draw or construct a medieval castle after researching information on its physical features. Have them add labels showing these features.

Record and present information in a variety of ways.

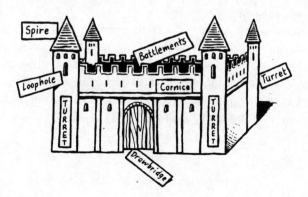

- List all the traditional fairy tales (known to the children) that feature a king, queen, princess and/or prince. Discuss how the characters are portrayed and follow particular stereotypes. Read *Jane and the Dragon* by Martin Baynton. Compare the character roles of the princess and prince in this book with those in traditional tales. Encourage the children to write their own fairy tale where the main characters do not fit the usual stereotypes.
- Discuss the gifts that the fairy godmothers bestowed on the princess at her naming ceremony and the fact that they were not material gifts. Ask the children to imagine that they are a fairy godmother/father — what special gift would they give to a baby girl/boy? Have them write and display their gift on a star.

- Ask the children to put themselves in the position of being the only fairy who the king and queen did not invite to the naming ceremony. Have them write a letter to a friend (another wicked fairy) explaining why they felt angry and describing their actions at the ceremony.
- Revisit the text and explore the language used to describe some of the actions of the characters. Write these phrases onto cards and ask the children to explain or act out the meaning of each. Have them then match the cards to the characters.

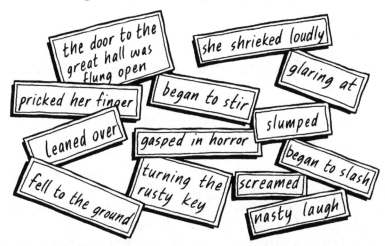

- One hundred years have passed since the princess fell asleep. Discuss the changes she would notice if she were to wake up in the year 2100. Invite the children to draw an illustration of Sleeping Beauty. Have them create speech and thought bubbles around the princess describing her observations and feelings.
- Revisit the tale. Turn to p.21 and have the children use the play format. Encourage each child to take on a character role and practise their part using appropriate intonation and expression. Have the children produce the play using a variety of technologies, e.g. make a tape recording of the play (including sound effects). Set up a listening post in the classroom so that other children (or other classes) can listen to or read along with the play. As an extension, locate other versions of the story for the children to listen to.

Books to share and compare

- *The Paper Bag Princess,*
  Robert Munsch,
  Scholastic, 1989.
- *Jane and the Dragon,*
  Martin Baynton,
  Scholastic, 1988.
- *The Frog Princess,*
  retold by Carol Krueger,
  Shortland Publications, 1993.
- *Cinderella,*
  retold by Barbara Karlin,
  Little and Brown, 1989.
- *Cinderella,*
  retold by Beverley Randell,
  PM Traditional Tales and Plays
  Gold Level,
  Nelson ITP, 1999.
- *Snow White and the Seven Dwarfs,*
  retold by Beverley Randell,
  PM Traditional Tales and Plays
  Gold Level,
  Nelson ITP, 1999.
- *Beauty and the Beast,*
  retold by Annette Smith,
  PM Traditional Tales and Plays
  Gold Level,
  Nelson ITP, 1999.

Richard Whittington was Lord Mayor of London in 1397, 1406 and 1419, in the reigns of Henry IV and Henry V. The familiar story about his early struggles as a boy in London was not written down for another two centuries. No one knows which parts of the tale are true and which are embroidery.

Setting: London and Morocco

Era: about 1370

Dick Whittington

Creating the atmosphere

- Read *Puss-in-Boots* (PM Traditional Tales and Plays Purple Level). Discuss how Puss helped his master, a miller's son, to make his fortune.

Focusing on the tale — guided reading

- Explain that *Dick Whittington*, like *Puss-in-Boots*, is also about a cat and its master. After the tale has been read by the class, invite the children to compare the two stories.
- Invite the children to read the title and discuss the cover and title page illustrations.
- pp.2–3 — Ask the children to read these pages silently to establish the period of time in which the story is set and the general setting. Ask them to list on a chart the characteristics of the main character, Dick. This list can be added to as the children read and gather more information. Discuss why people wanted to go to the big 'town' of London.
- pp.4–7 — Ask the children to skim read these pages and identify the names of the characters. They can then go back and read the story carefully. Ask the children to:
  — talk about the story plot and why Dick is so hungry
  — describe the characters of Mr Fitzwarren, Miss Alice and the cook, and then re-read the text to locate the author's descriptions of these characters
  — discuss the meanings of the words *exhausted*, *merchant*, *attic*, *bad-tempered*.
- pp.8–11 — Direct the children to read these pages independently to find out why, at first, Dick is so happy and then why he becomes sad. Discuss the value of the money Dick earned, what Dick bought with his penny and what 'making your fortune' means. Ensure that the children understand the term *mouser*.
- pp.12–13 — Explain the term *milestone* and ask the children why Dick might be sitting there. Have them read p.12 to confirm or re-evaluate their suggestions. Ask the children why this illustration is important, as it is also on the front cover.
- pp.14–17 — Discuss the contrast between the setting (and the costumes) on pp.14–15 with Dick's room on pp.8–9. Have the children predict what might happen to the rats feasting on the food. Ask them to read these pages independently. Discuss the meanings of the words *dismayed*, *plagued*, *swarmed*, *overjoyed*. Using an atlas, locate the continent of Africa and encourage the children to predict the journey that the cat may have taken from London.
- pp.18–20 — Have the children read these pages to find out how everyone benefited from Dick's cat. Relate the tale's ending to other tales the children know where the main characters get married and everyone lives happily ever after.

Going beyond the tale

- Compare *Puss-in-Boots* with *Dick Whittington*. Discuss the similarities and differences between the two tales. Have the children write their suggestions onto strips of card and paste these onto a chart under the headings 'Similarities' and 'Differences'.
- Collect a range of stories where a cat is the hero or main character of the story. Encourage the children to read and enjoy these books. Have them keep a

Provide opportunities for the children to express their ideas and opinions orally.

reading log of the stories they read. They could then select one story and share with the rest of the class why the cat is the hero.

- Dick makes his fortune and becomes a wealthy man. Have the children place this scenario into today's society. Direct the children to take on the role of a newspaper reporter and have them interview Dick, Lord Mayor of London. They will need to construct appropriate questions and role-play the interview. They can then write an article about Dick under an appropriate and eye-catching newspaper heading. Ensure that the children have time to discuss the role of a newspaper reporter, the purpose and format of an interview, and the purpose and structure of a newspaper article.

- The king and queen rewarded the ship's captain with gold and jewels. Invite the children to make necklaces, crowns, bracelets and rings from card, buttons and beads. They can construct a casket to hold the jewels.

- The palace provided a wonderful feast for their visitors. Have the children design a menu for the feast. Ask them to revisit the text and in particular, refer to the visual information. Encourage them to consider the selection of food and the number of courses needed to make a feast fit for a king and queen. Have the children look at a variety of menus, noting the layout, use of various fonts, organisational structure and the language used. Ask each child to design and make an attractive menu. Share these with the class.

- Take the children to visit the school library for the purpose of finding books about sailing ships that were used for trading with Northern Africa in the 14th century. If possible, have them find out what the ships were made of, how they were sailed, and what cargo they carried to and from their destinations.

- Revisit the tale. Turn to p.21 and organise the children to use the play format. Each child can take on a character role and practise their part using appropriate intonation and expression. Have the children produce the play using a variety of technologies, e.g. they could dress up in costume and make the masks provided on pp.31–32. Encourage them to video their performance in order to critically view their actions and make appropriate changes.

Communicate ideas using drama.

Books to share and compare

- *Tim All Alone,*
  Edward Ardizzone,
  Oxford University Press, 1971.
- *The Gardener,*
  Sarah Stewart,
  Farrar, Straus & Giroux, 1997.
- *Catkin,*
  Antonia Barber,
  Walker Books, 1994.
- *The Mousehole Cat,*
  Antonia Barber,
  Walker Books, 1990.

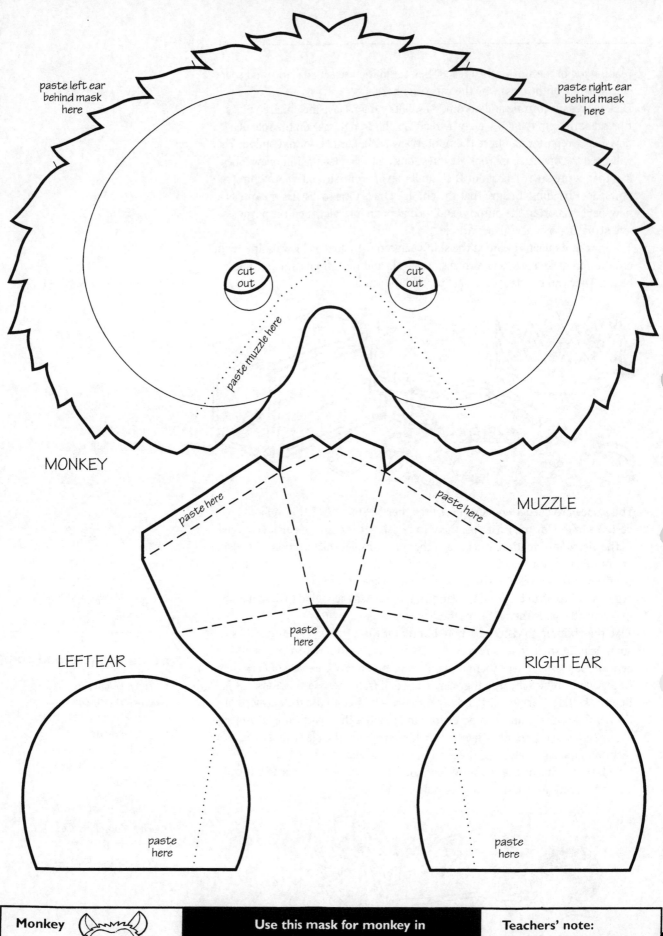

paste left ear
behind mask
here

paste right ear
behind mask
here

cut
out

cut
out

paste muzzle here

MONKEY

paste here

paste here

MUZZLE

paste
here

LEFT EAR

RIGHT EAR

paste
here

paste
here

PM Traditional Tales and Plays Teachers' Guide Silver Level (Set D)

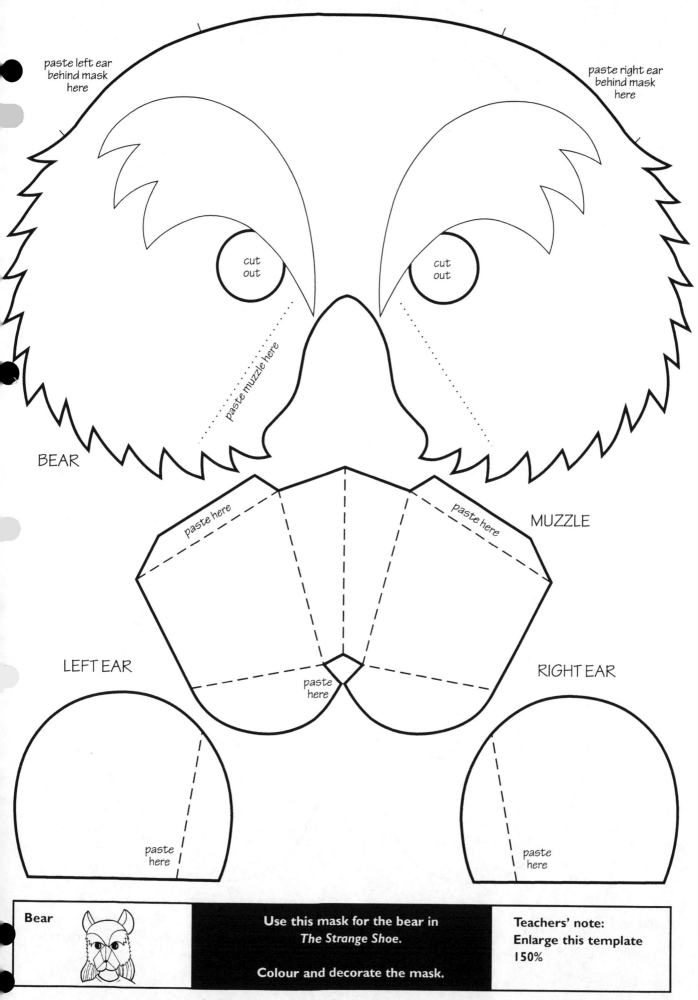

paste left ear
behind mask
here

paste right ear
behind mask
here

cut
out

cut
out

paste muzzle here

BEAR

paste here

paste here

MUZZLE

paste
here

LEFT EAR

RIGHT EAR

paste
here

paste
here

Bear

Use this mask for the bear in
The Strange Shoe.

Colour and decorate the mask.

Teachers' note:
**Enlarge this template
150%**

PM Traditional Tales and Plays Teachers' Guide Silver Level (Set D)

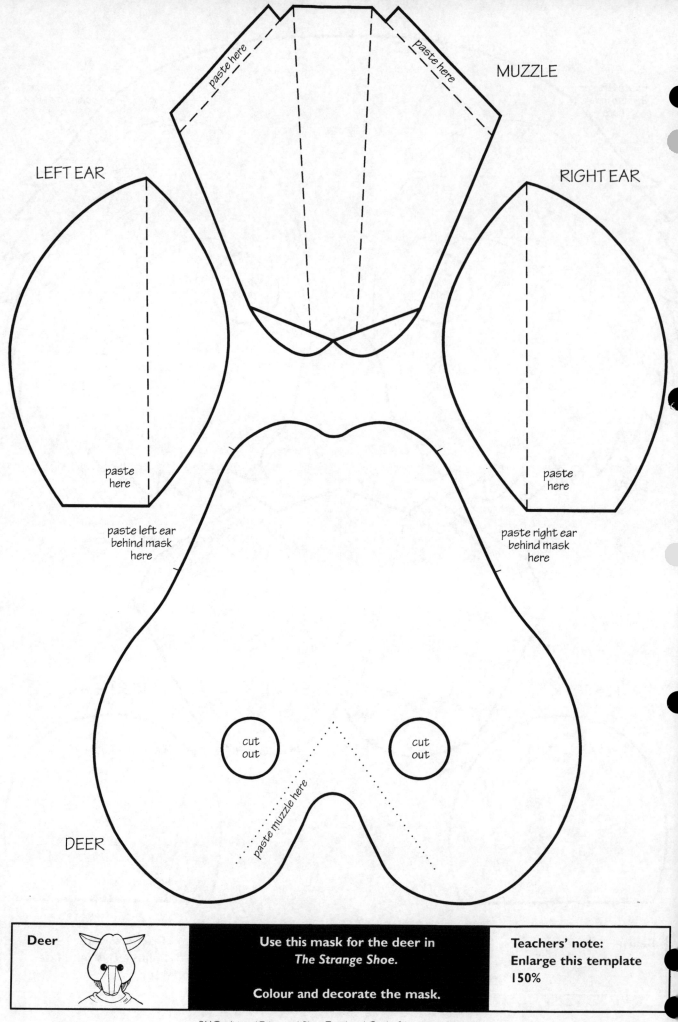

MUZZLE

paste here

paste here

LEFT EAR

RIGHT EAR

paste
here

paste
here

paste left ear
behind mask
here

paste right ear
behind mask
here

cut
out

cut
out

paste muzzle here

DEER

Deer

Use this mask for the deer in
The Strange Shoe.

Colour and decorate the mask.

Teachers' note:
**Enlarge this template
150%**

PM Traditional Tales and Plays Teachers' Guide Silver Level (Set D)

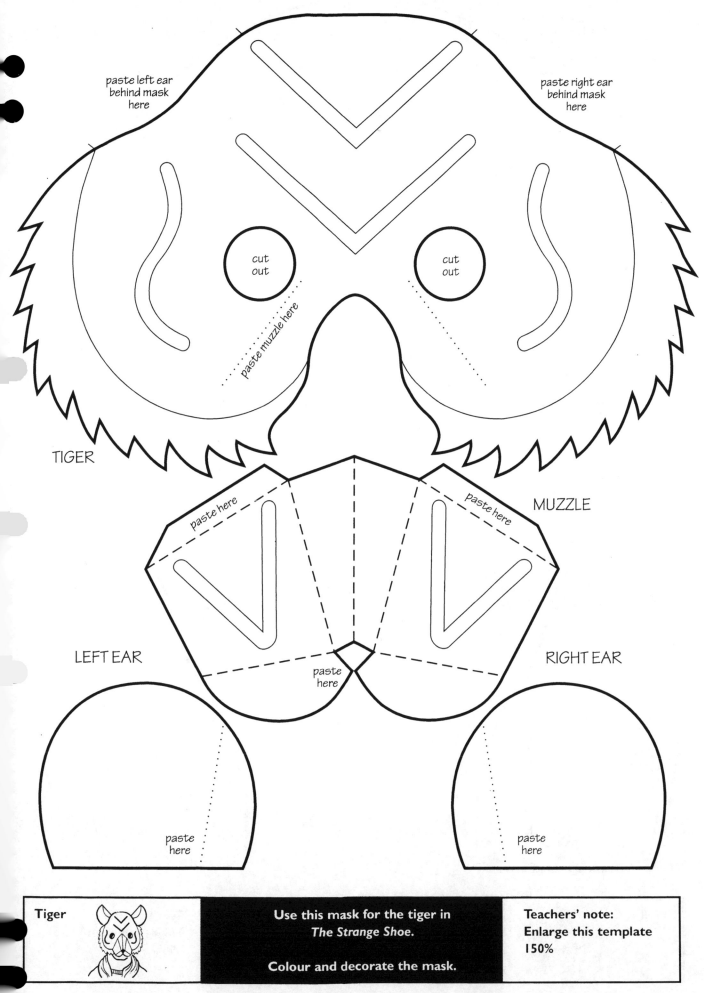

paste left ear
behind mask
here

paste right ear
behind mask
here

cut
out

cut
out

paste muzzle here

TIGER

MUZZLE

paste here

paste here

paste
here

LEFT EAR

RIGHT EAR

paste
here

paste
here

Tiger

Use this mask for the tiger in
The Strange Shoe.

Colour and decorate the mask.

Teachers' note:
**Enlarge this template
150%**

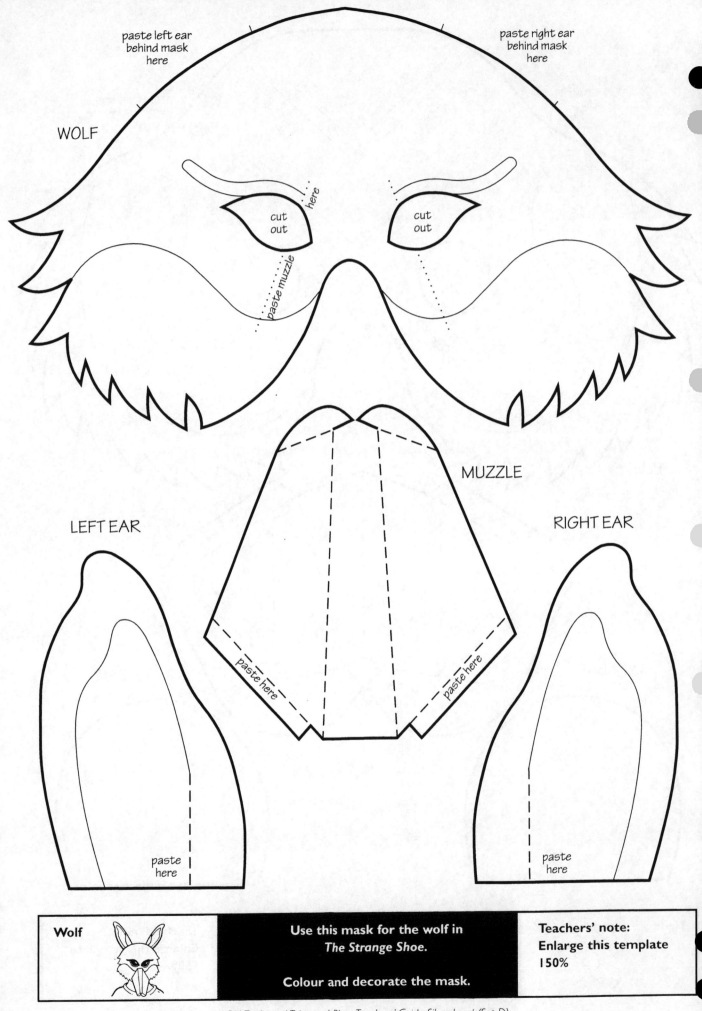

WOLF

paste left ear
behind mask
here

paste right ear
behind mask
here

here

cut
out

cut
out

paste muzzle

MUZZLE

LEFT EAR

RIGHT EAR

paste here

paste here

paste
here

paste
here

Wolf

Use this mask for the wolf in
The Strange Shoe.

Colour and decorate the mask.

**Teachers' note:
Enlarge this template
150%**

PM Traditional Tales and Plays Teachers' Guide Silver Level (Set D)

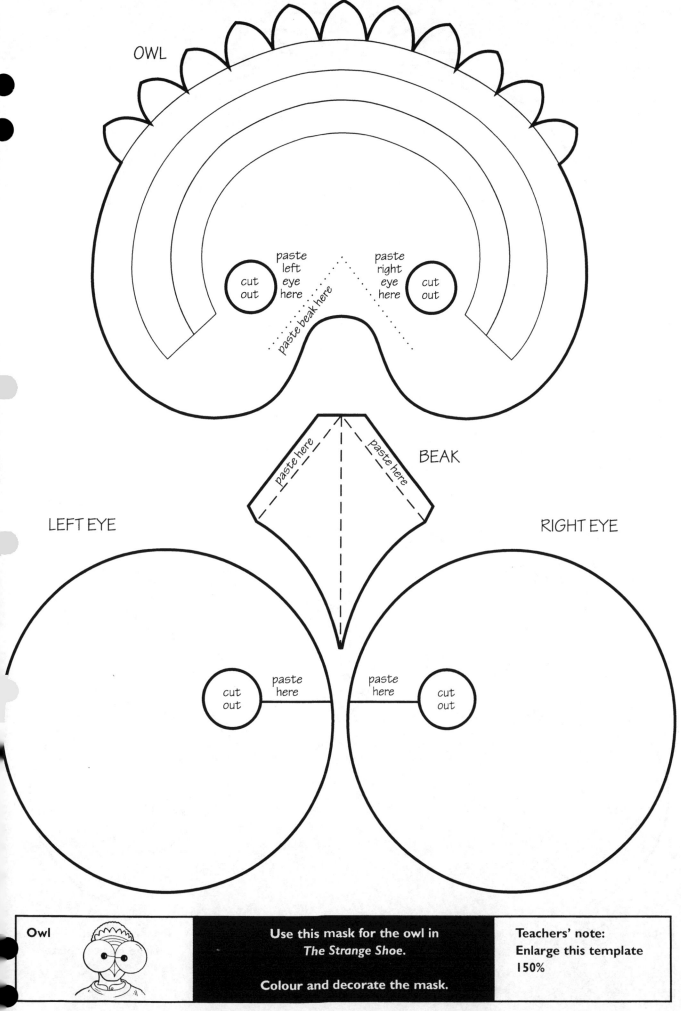

OWL

paste
left
eye
here

cut
out

paste
right
eye
here

cut
out

paste beak here

BEAK

paste here

paste here

LEFT EYE

RIGHT EYE

cut
out

paste
here

paste
here

cut
out

Owl

Use this mask for the owl in
The Strange Shoe.

Colour and decorate the mask.

Teachers' note:
**Enlarge this template
150%**

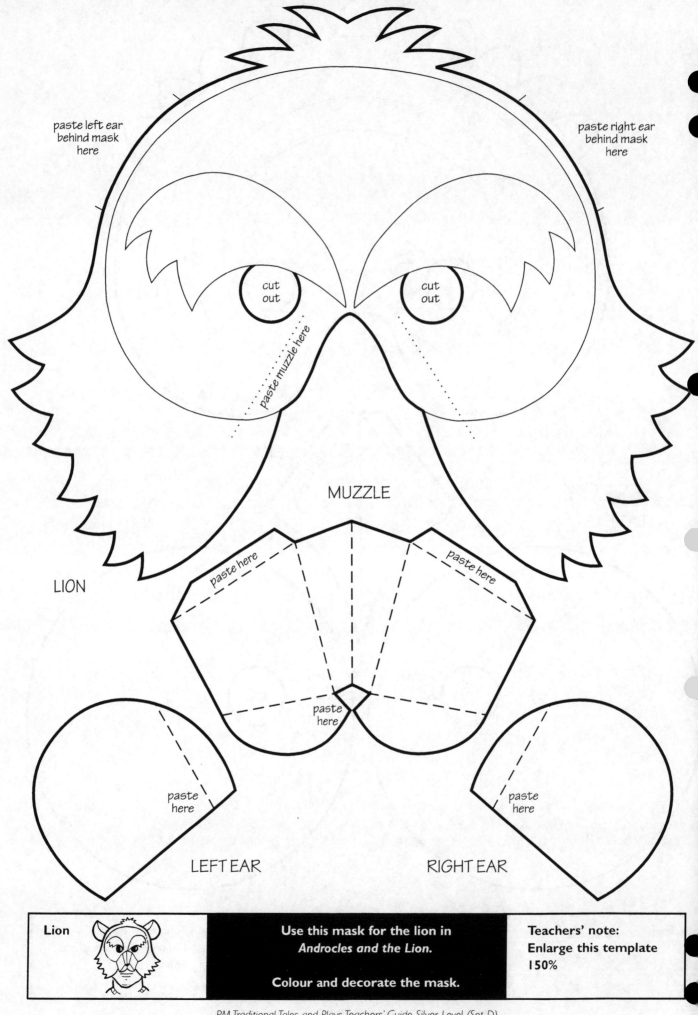

paste left ear
behind mask
here

paste right ear
behind mask
here

cut
out

cut
out

paste muzzle here

MUZZLE

LION

paste here

paste here

paste
here

LEFT EAR

RIGHT EAR

paste
here

paste
here

Lion

**Use this mask for the lion in
*Androcles and the Lion.***

Colour and decorate the mask.

**Teachers' note:
Enlarge this template
150%**

PM Traditional Tales and Plays Teachers' Guide Silver Level (Set D)

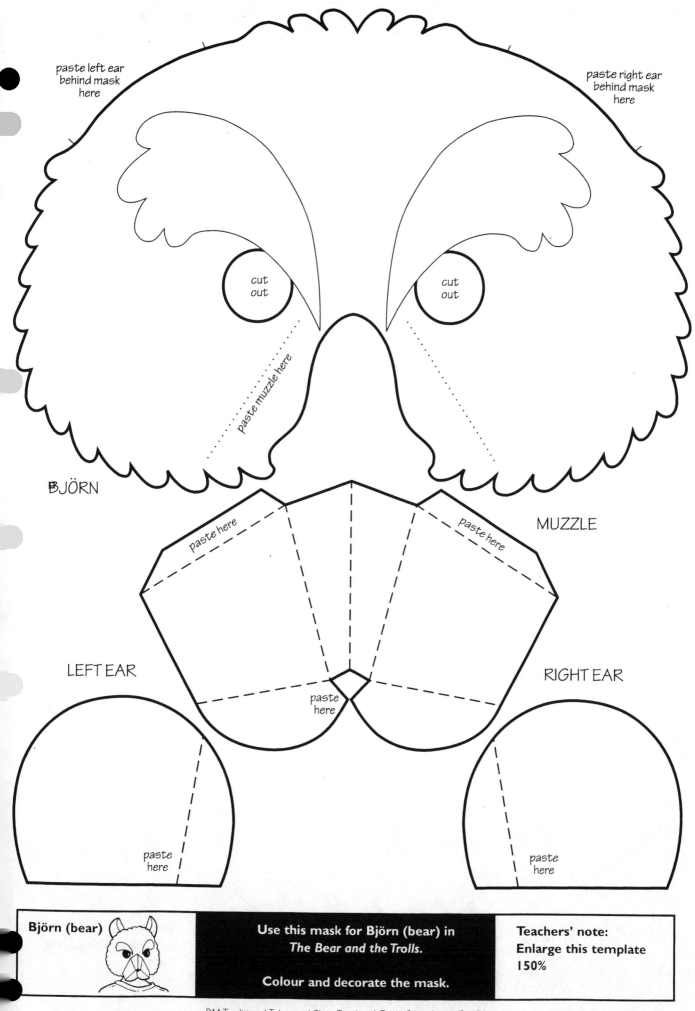

paste left ear
behind mask
here

paste right ear
behind mask
here

cut
out

cut
out

paste muzzle here

BJÖRN

MUZZLE

paste here

paste here

paste
here

LEFT EAR

RIGHT EAR

paste
here

paste
here

Björn (bear)

Use this mask for Björn (bear) in
The Bear and the Trolls.

Colour and decorate the mask.

Teachers' note:
Enlarge this template
150%

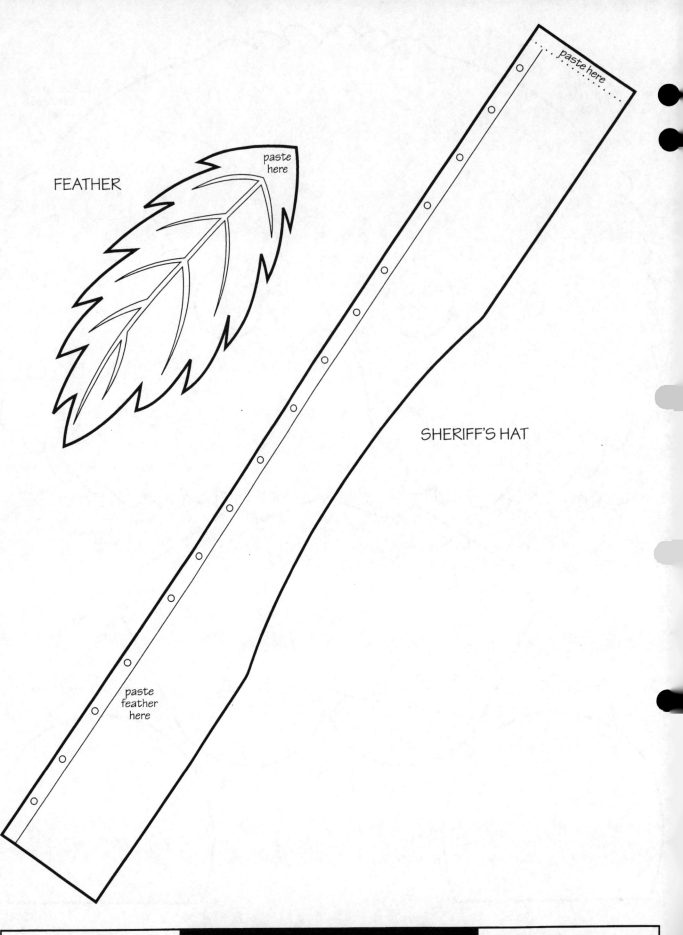

FEATHER

paste here

paste here

SHERIFF'S HAT

paste feather here

Sherriff's hat	Use this template for the sheriff's hat in *Robin Hood and the Silver Trophy*. Colour and decorate the template.	Teachers' note: Enlarge this template 150%

KING'S CROWN

paste here

King's crown	Use this template for the king's crown in *The Sleeping Beauty*. **Colour and decorate the template.**	Teachers' note: **Enlarge this template 150%**

PM Traditional Tales and Plays Teachers' Guide Silver Level (Set D)

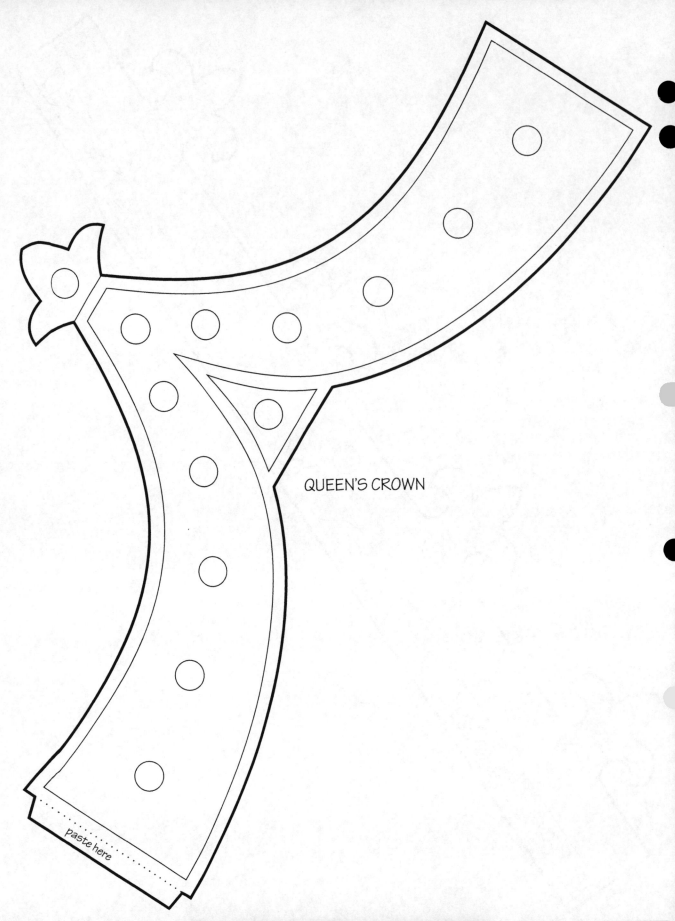

QUEEN'S CROWN

paste here

Queen's crown    **Use this template for the queen's crown in** *The Sleeping Beauty.*   **Teachers' note: Enlarge this template 150%**

Colour and decorate the template.

PM Traditional Tales and Plays Teachers' Guide Silver Level (Set D)

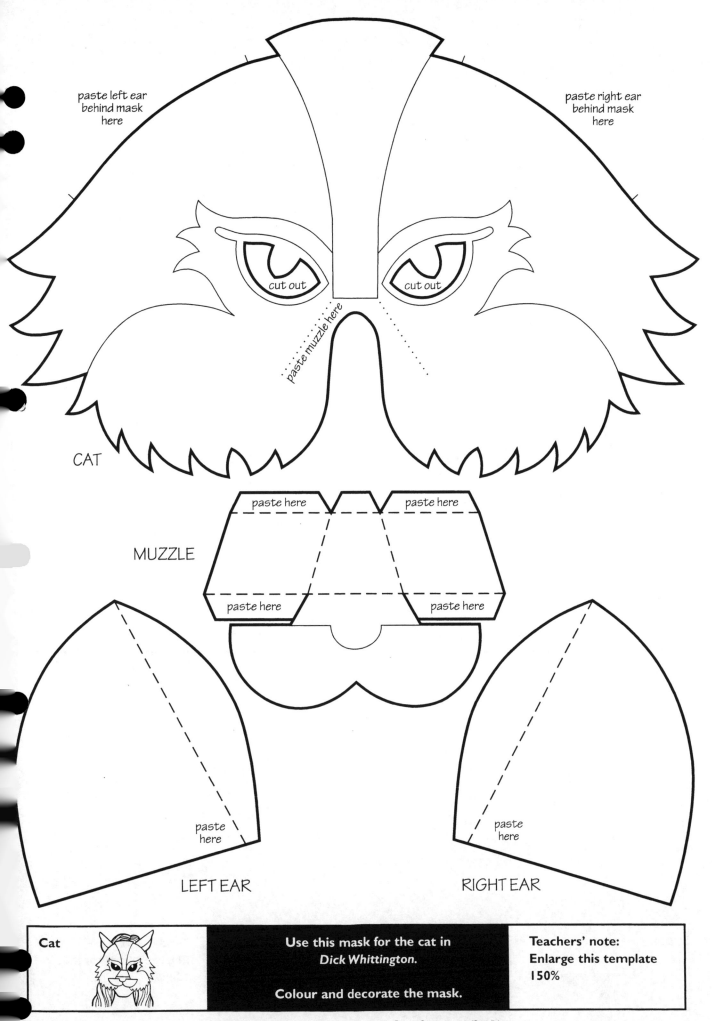

paste left ear
behind mask
here

paste right ear
behind mask
here

cut out

cut out

paste muzzle here

CAT

MUZZLE

paste here

paste here

paste here

paste here

LEFT EAR

paste
here

RIGHT EAR

paste
here

Cat

Use this mask for the cat in
Dick Whittington.

Colour and decorate the mask.

Teachers' note:
**Enlarge this template
150%**

PM Traditional Tales and Plays Teachers' Guide Silver Level (Set D)
© Nelson Thomson Learning, 2000. This page may be photocopied for educational use within the purchasing institution.

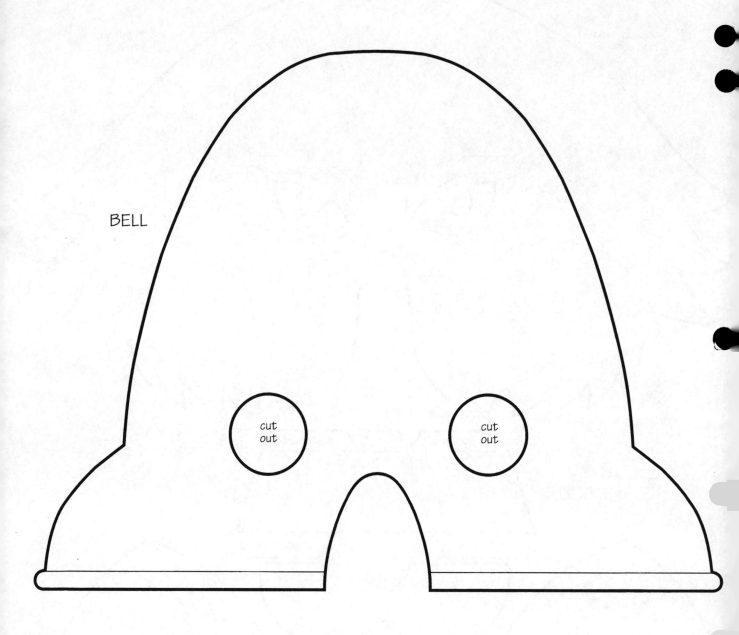

BELL

cut
out

cut
out

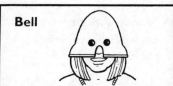

Bell

Use this template for the bell in
Dick Whittington.

Colour and decorate the mask.

Teachers' note:
Enlarge this template
150%

PM Traditional Tales and Plays Teachers' Guide Silver Level (Set D)